t/ l2

Where We Once Gathered

Lost Synagogues of Europe

Eifrig Publishing LLC

Lemont   Berlin

Published by Eifrig Publishing,
PO Box 66, 701 Berry Street, Lemont, PA 16851, USA
Knobelsdorffstr. 44, 14059 Berlin, Germany.

For information regarding permission, write to:
Rights and Permissions Department,
Eifrig Publishing,
PO Box 66, 701 Berry Street, Lemont, PA 16851, USA.
permissions@eifrigpublishing.com, +1-888-340-6543

Library of Congress Control Number: 2011942360

 Strongwater, Andrea
Where We Once Gathered, Lost Synagogues of Europe/
written and illustrated by Andrea Strongwater

p. cm.

Paperback: ISBN 978-1-936172-48-1
Hard cover: ISBN 978-1-936172-49-8

[1. Jewish History – Juvenile non-fiction.
2. Holocaust – Juvenile non-fiction.]

I. Strongwater, Andrea, ill. II. Title

16 15 14 13 2012
5 4 3 2 1

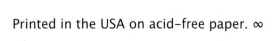

Printed in the USA on acid-free paper. ∞   www.astrongwater.com

Where We Once Gathered

Lost Synagogues of Europe

paintings and words by

Andrea Strongwater

Why this Book?

An essay for the reader

The European cities represented by the synagogues in this book were, prior to the Holocaust, the center of the modern Jewish world. Jews in each of these communities were part of the fabric of daily life, though often relegated to the fringes of this tapestry by the undercurrent of antisemitism, which permeated Europe for centuries.

Since the Diaspora, Jewish communities throughout the world have always taken on aspects of their new homes. Jews adopted the language, manner, and even the art and architecture of their neighbors. They worked among the general population, being welcomed as physicians, intellectuals, shopkeepers, and, yes, moneylenders; yet when they returned home, that home was on the *Judengasse*, the "Jew Street," or in the Jewish quarter. On that street, in that quarter, was a synagogue or, often, several synagogues, which mirrored the details and style of the church or cathedral nearby. Externally, the Jew may have looked like his neighbor, but inside his synagogue and in his soul, he was most assuredly different.

Jewish communities often easily accepted this segregation. In part, it met their need to be near their synagogue in the established Eruv [sacred community] where they could move freely and maintain normal activities on the Sabbath or holidays. So then, even if not required by local law, the Jewish community would isolate itself around the central symbol of their community – the synagogue. This was the center of that community, acting as temple for worship, a Shul [school] for the children's education, as a court to settle civil matters, as a meeting place for the elders to discuss matters of religious observance, and the location of all manner of celebrations.

The Nazis' Final Solution rendered many of these towns and cities *Judenrein* [free of Jews]. When the Allies prevailed and World War II ended, thousands of synagogues and 6,000,000 Jews were destroyed, wiped from the face of Europe, their home for centuries.

Certainly, the Nazis allowed some synagogue buildings and ritual objects to be maintained to teach future generations about a lost race (many valuable objects also found their way into the private collections of high-ranking Nazi Party members). Most of the synagogues themselves, however, were purposely destroyed: razed to the ground or dismantled, often by the Jews themselves, forced to do so under threat of death. It is worth noticing that there were places where the town leaders stood up to the SS and the soldiers, and the synagogues survived; there is at least one instance where the local (non-Jewish) supervisor of the dismantling of a synagogue defied orders and removed the stones to one place where they were buried, to be recovered someday to rebuild.

Lost Synagogues? They are lost only if we forget. How can we even begin to discuss what was lost until we know what was before. Strongwater's paintings evoke the beauty and vitality of the lost communities of Europe. Just like the 6,000,000 Jews murdered, the synagogues and the communities that they represent must be remembered. Families worked, lived, learned and loved in these diverse places. Blacksmiths and teachers, tailors and doctors, beggars and moguls, mothers, fathers, and children created communities in every sense of that word – communities that centered around the ubiquitous, often imposing (though sometimes humble) structures shown in *Where We Once Gathered, Lost Synagogues of Europe*.

Stephen M. Goldman, Executive Director
Holocaust Memorial Center, Zekelman Family Campus
Detroit, Michigan

Acknowledgements

Many people have helped me with this project and I thank them all. Most importantly I thank Roger Tamraz, who saw the significance of this work when it was four paintings and an idea. He has supported the project in every way possible. For help with research, I thank Sharon Mintz at the Jewish Theological Seminary in New York, the US Holocaust Memorial Museum in Washington, D.C., and Bill Gross of Tel Aviv, who offered me a treasure trove of archival photos to work with. Thanks to the estate of Frances Siegelbaum, which funded the creation of a formal book proposal that turned my collection of paintings and research into book format. Thanks to Ronnie Wachsler, who maintains an ongoing display of my artwork at Bagels & Co on the Upper West Side of Manhattan, and to Valerie Armento, Ruth Becker, Sharon and Stanley Clavir, David Hammerstein, Congregation Edmond J. Safra, Alicia Sainer and Richard Morgan, L. David and Rana Silver, Phyliss Silver, Pauline Stillman and my old friend Larry Stillman, who has mapped the cities in my project. I thank Kathy Frankovic and Hal Glatzer for making the re-creation of the synagogue in Glatz possible. I greatly appreciate the interest and generosity they have shown all along the way. I thank the guys in the map room at Olin Library at Cornell University, Lydia Fakundiny, and Cornell University in all its parts – a place where I have always found and will continue to find instruction in any study.

A. S.

Many of the locations in this collection have been part of different countries at different times. For this project, the place names are listed according to the international borders of 1935.

From the Artist

My perspective as an artist regarding "The Lost Synagogues of Europe" is also the subject of a long essay I am writing to be included in the coffee table book version of the project. In a nutshell, what I am doing is telling a part of Jewish history that I have missed hearing. It's a way for me to connect the dots.

My mother's family came to the US from Poland in 1926. My grandfather had packed a bag several times in the early 1920s and gone in search of a better place to be a Jew. He decided that America was the only safe place, even if it wasn't necessarily the most sympathetic. As the head of a large family and one of many siblings, he helped get everyone here to the USA. As soon as he could, he obtained US citizenship and passports for everyone. He sent those passports to Europe to be doctored and used to get more Jews out. He worked hard to establish Israel and cherished the photo he had of himself with David Ben Gurion. He and the rest of my mother's family were very active in helping refugees before and after the war, here in the US and elsewhere. My mother was a regional vice president of Women's American ORT, and there is even a school somewhere in Israel with my father's name on the wall. It always seemed important to me to make a contribution.

When my grandmother died, Sarah, a very glamorous German Jewish woman, came into my grandfather's life. She looked him up when she found out my grandmother died. Although she didn't discuss it very much, she told me that the only reason she survived the war was that my grandfather supported her and her sons in hiding and that he did that for many people. We sang Hatikvah when we lit the Hanukah candles – the menorah had a music box in the base – and my grandfather cried as he always did when emotions got the better of him. We spent every Sabbath at my grandparent's tiny house in the Bronx, New York, where many of his siblings came to discuss politics, art, and Israel. My friends asked each other if we were Jews first or Americans first. We watched Gertrude Berg on TV and my grandmother actually talked to her neighbor through their kitchen windows, just like Molly Goldberg.

The father of the boy who sat next to me in high school wrote "Fiddler on the Roof," which my grandfather insisted we all watch, as he, like one of the characters, was the first in his neighborhood in Poland to get a sewing machine. We used William L. Shirer's "Rise and Fall of the Third Reich" to learn the story of WWII. My mother and I always agreed that the horror of the war made it impossible to think. All we could do was cry. So how do you tell the story? And how do you account for the sophistication of my multi-lingual, world-traveling grandparents?

For me, this project illuminates what came before the war – something that was not talked about much when I was younger. I understand the pain that made that a reality, but as time goes on and I learn more, I think we should all know more about what the Jewish culture created and maintained.

I tell the story in a visceral way that speaks through pictures and the accretion of small details – one synagogue after another, some very similar in architectural style, each story having some unique aspect. One synagogue hosted Zionist meetings, another was the first Reform synagogue with an organ, which was paid for by a court Jew, another had an organ that was never used on the Sabbath. Jews arrived in these places as early as the Roman Legions in the first century A.D. The synagogues served as centers of Jewish life, not just to pray but also to hear the latest gossip or a lecture, see art, hear concert music and of course hold weddings, bar mitzvahs, holiday and ritual events of Jewish life. All the synagogues in my project (except Turin) were totally erased. That fact states the reality of the Holocaust, although I have chosen not to delve into the details.

I present, through my paintings, the glory of what existed before the Holocaust.

Andrea Strongwater

8

Tübingen, Germany

In 1882, the small Jewish community in Tübingen and Reutlingen built this synagogue. At the inauguration of the synagogue on December 8, 1882, Dr. Michael Silberstein, the District Rabbi, made the following prayer:

May You, G-d, as You promised, be close to all Your children, not only towards the brother in faith, but also towards the brother in mankind, answer his prayers, in whatever language he is praying to you, have mercy on him, from whichever people he comes, for you had once spoken: My house shall be named Congregation House for all peoples.

At the beginning of the 20th century, it had about 100 members and employed a cantor, but not a rabbi. On Kristallnacht, November 9–10, 1938, the district chief of Tübingen ordered Nazi SA and SS men to destroy the synagogue. The Jewish community was forced to pay for the removal of the debris.

Dortmund, Germany

The first Jews were recorded in Dortmund in the 13th century. This synagogue, called the Great Synagogue, was designed by Eduard von Furstenau and built on Hiltropwall in 1900. It was forcibly sold to the Nazis before Kristallnacht.

In the 1930s, antisemitic laws severely reduced income for the Jewish community, often making it impossible for them to maintain their institutions. Their last resort was then to sell their buildings at greatly deflated prices to the local government – as occurred in Dortmund.

This synagogue was destroyed by the Nazis in September 1938, as a test to see how the local population would react. It was completely removed sometime before November 1938. Nothing remains of the building. The site is now a public square with a memorial stone and picture of the synagogue.

10

11

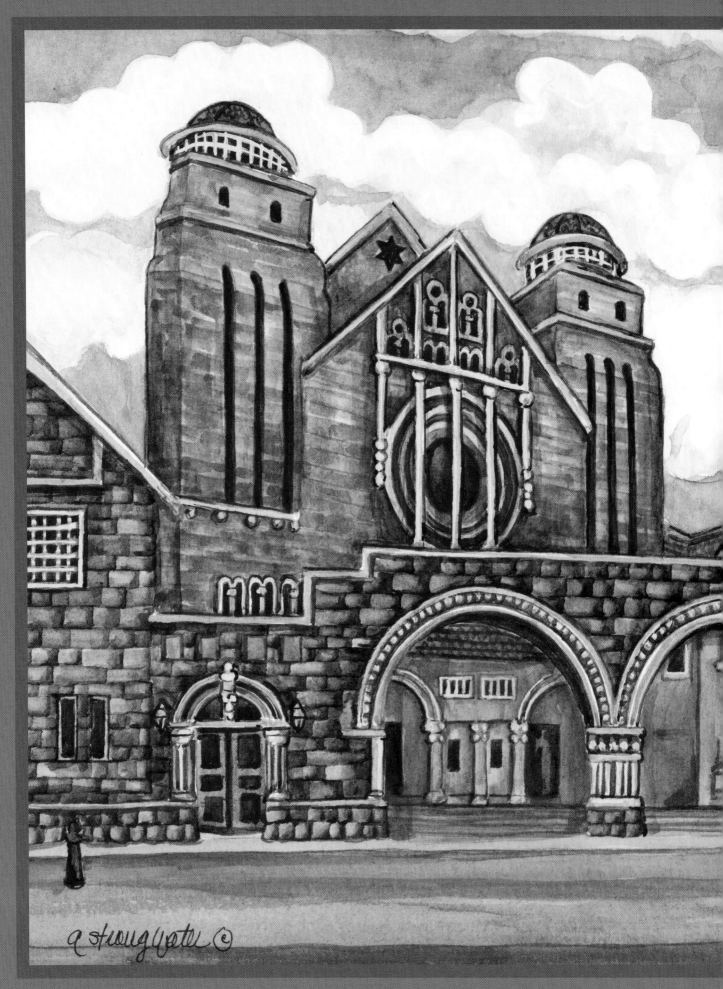

a stroughater ©

Frankfurt am Main, Germany

The *Israelitische Religions-gesellschaft* Synagogue

The design for this synagogue was selected through a contest, won by architects Peter Jurgensen and Jurgen Bachman in 1904. The group that established this synagogue was part of an organization founded in 1848 to champion Orthodox Judaism. It had the financial support of the Rothschild family and was an important influence in the Agudath Israel organization, founded in 1912.

During Kristallnacht, the night of November 9–10, 1938, the Nazis destroyed the building by setting fires and detonating explosives. From 1942–1943, using forced labor, the Nazis built an air raid shelter on the site, which was recently renovated and upgraded to an ABC civil bunker.

Bochum, Germany

Bochum is located in the Rhine-Westphalia region of Germany near Hanover. Jews were first recorded living in Bochum in 1349. Almost six hundred years later, in 1933, there were 1,152 Jews supporting two synagogues, a cheder, a Hebrew School, eight benevolent societies, and cultural organizations.

On Kristallnacht, the main synagogue was set on fire and allowed to burn to the ground. Bochum, along with neighboring Herne and Recklinghausen, has seen a post-WWII influx of Jews from eastern Europe. A new synagogue was erected in Recklinghausen in 1955, and in 2007, another was inaugurated in Bochum.

Kristallnacht

Kristallnacht is also known as The Night of Broken Glass. On the night of November 9 and continuing into November 10, 1938, the Nazis destroyed hundreds of Jewish synagogues, sacked, looted, and burned thousands of Jewish shops, and removed tens of thousands of Jews from their communities and brought them to concentration camps. This pogrom was named Kristallnacht because of the huge amount of glass that was smashed all over Germany and German-controlled lands. Kristallnacht marked a turning point in the world's perception of Hitler's Nazi party.

Seesen, Germany

The Jacobson Tempel was the first one built specifically for Reform services. It was dedicated in July 1810 and was paid for and endowed by Israel Jacobson, a financier and Court Jew. It was meant to embody Jacobson's reform ideas to liberate Jews from their past and connect them with the local Christian community.

The synagogue had bells, a choir, and organ – things that no Orthodox synagogue would have. Other German Jewish communities adopted the Reform movement, creating serious disputes between Reformist and Orthodox Jews. Many of the Reform movement's leaders immigrated to the United States, where the movement took hold.

On Kristallnacht, November 9–10, 1938, the synagogue was set on fire and totally destroyed. A new building has been erected on the site that includes a memorial stone with an inscription about the synagogue.

18

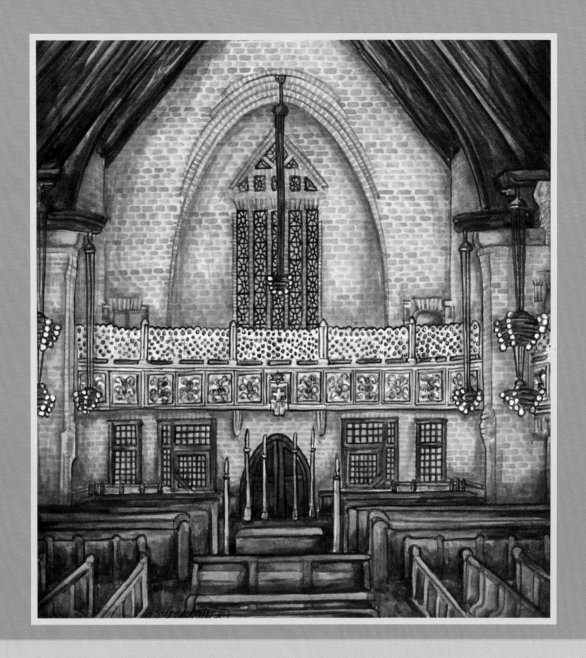

Amsterdam, The Netherlands

This synagogue was built on Linnaeusstraat and inaugurated on September 6, 1928. Jacob Baars, a Jewish architect, designed it in the style of the Amsterdam School. Leo Pinkhof created the beautiful and important stained glass windows for the synagogue. The complex included a mikveh and community meeting spaces. It was designed for 300 families with seating for 334 men and 114 women. The contractors and workers were Jewish.

The interior was heavily damaged and looted during WWII. There were no services held after 1956 and the building was demolished in 1962. The copper grillwork and stained glass were sent to Ramat Gan in Israel.

Livorno, Italy

There has been a synagogue on this site since the 1500s, when the ruler of Livorno invited Jews to settle here and create businesses. In 1927, the synagogue housed Italy's first museum of Hebrew art.

The building was enlarged and upgraded throughout the centuries until its destruction during WWII. A new synagogue is now located on this site.

Luxembourg

Count Siegfried founded Luxembourg in 963 CE. Luxembourg City is the capital of the country of Luxembourg. Jews have lived here since the late 1200s, always returning after being repeatedly expelled. In 1349, they were murdered or banished after being blamed for causing the Black Plague. In 1478, their homes were burned and many fled. They were expelled again in 1530. They always resettled, however. In 1808, there were approximately 75 Jews living in Luxembourg. The first synagogue was built in 1823. In the 1880s, the Jewish population grew to 87 families, and the synagogue pictured here was built.

During the Nazi occupation, which began in August 1940, *Gauleiter* (Nazi Party leader) Gustav Simon ordered the community erased. This synagogue was destroyed in 1943.

Strasbourg, Alsace, France

The Quai Kleber synagogue was inaugurated on September 8, 1898. Jews have lived in Strasbourg since the days of Charlemagne (over 1,000 years ago). Until the Crusades, they had their own legal codes, the right to own property and bear arms, freedom in commercial matters, and the right to be protected by local authorities.

The preaching for the First and Second Crusades in 1095 and 1146 blamed the Jews for many things. They were murdered in great numbers, even though the emperor and some higher level church dignitaries tried to protect them. Jews were alternately banished and welcomed through the 1700s.

In 1791, the National Assembly proclaimed the total emancipation of Jews living in France. The first synagogue in Strasbourg was built in 1809 on the Poêle des Drapiers. Another was built in 1836 and lasted until 1898, when it was replaced with the synagogue on Quai Kleber pictured here.

Strasbourg was home to many Jewish aid organizations, including a large hospital that was created in 1887, an orphanage for girls, and a Jewish school of arts and trades that was established in 1825. Before WWII, there were approximately 10,000 Jews living in Strasbourg.

During the Nazi occupation the synagogue was obliterated, with all remnants of it scattered and untraceable.

Przedbórz, Poland

This wooden synagogue was built around 1760. Its interior was one of the most ornately carved and painted of the wooden synagogues that were erected all over Poland. It had a single-barrel vault ceiling made out of intricately curved and interlocked strips of wood. Doors, capitals, bimah, and tzedakah were carved into patterns. The walls were covered in multi-colored depictions of Jerusalem, animals, floral motifs, and vines.

The synagogue was burned down when the Germans invaded during WWII.

Warsaw, Poland

The Great Synagogue of Warsaw on Tlomackie Street was built from 1875–1878 and was one of the largest synagogues in the world at the time. The architect was Leandro Marconi. The synagogue sat eleven hundred men and almost as many women. The bimah was in front with a choir loft for an 80-piece choir. The synagogue had an organ that was not used on the Sabbath. The liturgy was Orthodox. The cantorial custom of presenting prayers in an operatic fashion flourished here. Moshe Kouessivtsky, a famous cantor eventually made his way from Warsaw to New York, where he gave concerts in Brooklyn.

According to Alfred Döblin, a German Jewish visitor between the wars, *"...this was the synagogue of the middle class, also the enlightened, the emancipated, and the assimilated..."*

At 8:15 pm on May 16, 1943, to celebrate its victory over the Warsaw Ghetto uprising, the German army dynamited the building. *SS Gruppenführer* Jurgen Stroop recalled, *"What a wonderful sight! I called out 'Heil Hitler!' and pressed the button. A terrific explosion brought flames right up to the clouds. The colors were unbelievable. An unforgettable allegory of the triumph over Jewry. The Warsaw ghetto has ceased to exist. Because that is what Adolf Hitler and Heinrich Himmler wanted."*

Belz, Poland

Belz is a small town that was part of Poland from 1919 to 1939 and is currently located in western Ukraine. It had a large Hasidic community. This was their synagogue and study center, which opened in 1843. The Jewish community in Belz dates from the 14th century. In 1665, the Jews of Belz were given equal rights and duties of citizenship.

Before World War I, there were 6,100 inhabitants in Belz – more than half were Jewish. In late 1939, the Nazis invaded Belz and set about destroying the synagogue. Fire and dynamite were unsuccessful, and they finally conscripted Jewish men to take apart the three-foot walls brick by brick.

32

Łódź,
Poland

The Great Synagogue of Łódź was a Reform congregation located on what was then Spacerowa Street. Design and construction took place from around 1881 to 1887. The architect was Adolf Wolff, who designed many other large synagogues. This building was the biggest structure in central Łódź when it was finished. It was paid for by local industrialists, including Joachim Silberstein, Karol Scheibler, and Izrael Poznanski, who oversaw construction. The brother of industrialist Dawid Prussak is mentioned in the records as a founder of the synagogue.

On the night of November 14–15, 1939, the synagogue, including Torah scrolls and interior fixtures, was burned to the ground by Nazis. In 1940, the remains were removed. The site is now a parking lot.

Riga, Latvia

Jews are mentioned in Riga as far back as the 13th century. The Master of the German Order banned Jews from settling in the region in the 14th century. In 1561, Poland gained control of the area, and Jews began resettling. In the 15th and 16th centuries, some important Jews were allowed to live in Riga. In 1725, a Jewish cemetery was permitted. In the 18th century, rules regarding movement of Jews in and out of the city were relaxed, and the Jewish population of Riga increased. The first residents were skilled craftsmen including shoemakers, furriers, and furniture makers, intellectuals in finance, medicine, and law. The Jewish community was centered in a ghetto called Maskavas, which lies southeast of the Old Town. In the mid-1800s, housing restrictions were loosened, and many Jews moved to other parts of Riga.

In the late 1920s, Riga became the center of the Lubavitcher movement when Joseph Schneersohn received citizenship and protection from the Latvian government after being exiled from the Soviet Union.

The Great Choral Synagogue on Gogola Street, built from 1868–1871, was completely destroyed on July 4, 1941. Approximately 300 Jews were locked inside and grenades were thrown in through the windows to burn the building with everyone and everything inside. A memorial was dedicated on the site of the ruins on July 4, 1988.

Tartu, Estonia

There are reports of Jews in Estonia as early as the fourteenth century, even though Jews were forbidden from living there. Jewish settlement began in the nineteenth century after Tsar Alexander II, in an 1865 statute, granted Jews the right to enter the region. The Tartu congregation was formed in 1866 with fifty families. The heads of households were mostly small tradesmen and artisans and were mostly illiterate.

Tartu University opened to Jews in the late nineteenth century. The Republic of Estonia was established in 1918, and all peoples were tolerated. Cultural autonomy was a rare phenomenon in European history. The Estonian government was recognized by Jews worldwide. In 1920, the Macabi Sports Society was founded.

In 1940, the Soviets occupied Estonia and liquidated all cultural organizations as well as cultural autonomy. In 1941, the Germans invaded and murdered the remaining Jews.

Slavonski Brod, Croatia

Slavonski Brod is the largest city in Slavonia, the eastern part of Croatia. Jews settled here in the 7th century, where they lived until being expelled in 1456. In the late 1700s, Jews began to return, bringing the Jewish population to about 20,000 by the end of WWI. In 1941, Croatia and Bosnia-Herzegovina became the Independent State of Croatia ruled by the Ustase Party, which adhered to Nazi principles. Anti-Jewish laws ended Jewish rights, including the right to own property.

This synagogue was built in 1896 and destroyed in 1941. About two-thirds of the Jews were sent to concentration camps. In all, approximately 80% of the Jews of Croatia were murdered. Today there is a memorial plaque on the site of the synagogue.

40

Vienna, Austria
Heitzing Synagogue

The Heitzing Synagogue was built in the suburban XIII District of Vienna. There were two design competitions for this project, one in 1912 and another in 1924. Architects competing for the 1912 prize included Rudolf Perco, Ernst Lichtblau, and Hugo Gorge, among others. Plans exist of their designs, but the building was not erected. A second competition was held in 1924. Submitting architects included Fritz Landauer of Munich and Richard Neutra, who was then living in the United States. Judges included Josef Hoffman and three Viennese Jewish architects, who awarded the commission to Arthur Grunburger, a Viennese architect who had moved to California.

The synagogue was destroyed by the Nazis on Kristallnacht along with twenty-one others in Vienna. One synagogue was left standing – the *Stadttempel*, built in 1826 – because it was between buildings owned by gentiles that would have been damaged by a fire in the *Stadttempel*.

Vienna, Austria
Leopoldstädter Tempel

The *Israelitische Bethaus in der Wiener Vorstadt Leopoldstadt* was the largest synagogue of Vienna. It could seat 2,200 people with standing room for another 1,500, and it housed an important Jewish library. In August 1917, after a celebration for Emperor Karl I's birthday organized by Jewish soldiers, a fire severely damaged the building. The renovations were finished in 1921. In 1939, Jews had been living in Austria for 1,000 years.

A memorial plaque on the site reads: *"Here stood the Leopoldstädter Tempel, built in 1858 in Moorish style to the plans of Leopold Forster, and destroyed down to the foundations on Kristallnacht, November 10, 1938 by National Socialist barbarians."*

43

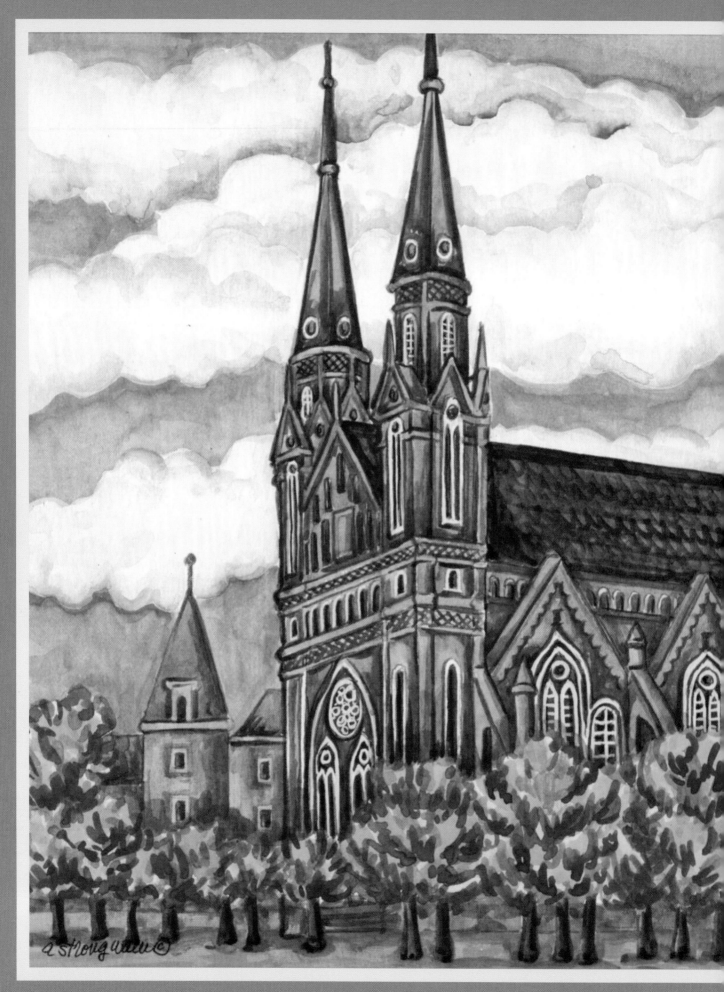

A. Strongwater©

České Budějovice, Czechoslovakia

České Budějovice, currently in the Czech Republic, is a center of manufacturing and particularly famous for its breweries – notably Budějovický Budvar (Budweiser). Max Fleischer, a culturally assimilated Jew, designed and built the synagogue in 1888. The Neo–Gothic building was meant to mimic Christian churches and send the message that Jews were just like everyone else in the country. The synagogue was part of the Reform movement and did not have a separate women's gallery. The exterior was red brick. The synagogue was dedicated on September 5, 1888.

On June 5, 1942, the Nazis set off an explosion to destroy the building. It is now an empty lot.

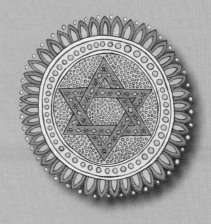

Karlovy Vary (Karlsbad), Czechoslovakia

In 1868, the Jewish community of Karlovy Vary received authorization to form a congregation. This synagogue, designed by Edwin Oppler to accommodate 2000 worshippers, was built in 1877. Karlovy Vary is a famous spa town that became a popular resort and meeting place for rabbis, communal leaders, and matchmakers. In 1847, a Prague philanthropic association established a hostel for needy Jewish patients visiting the town – the first institution of its kind. The 12th and 13th Zionist Congresses were held in Karlovy Vary in 1921 and 1923.

By 1930, the Jewish population was over 2,100, almost all of whom left during the Sudeten crisis of 1938. Jews are recorded in Karlovy Vary from the 13th century onwards. The synagogue was destroyed by the Nazis on Kristallnacht, November 9–10, 1938.

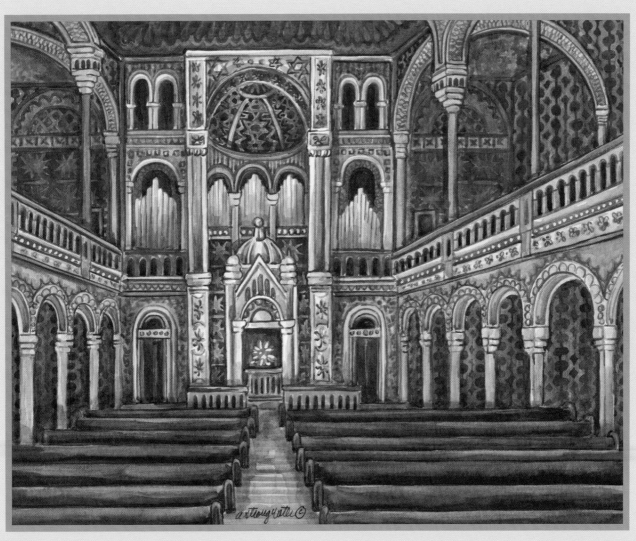

Index of Synagogues